ENGINEERING SUPER STRUCTURES

TUNNELS

PAIGE V. POLINSKY

Consulting Editor, Diane Craig, M.A./Reading Specialist

Sandcastle

An Imprint of Abdo Publishing
abdopublishing.com

abdopublishing.com

062017
092017

THIS BOOK CONTAINS
RECYCLED MATERIALS

Design: Kelly Doudna, Mighty Media, Inc.
Production: Mighty Media, Inc.
Editor: Rebecca Felix
Cover Photographs: Mighty Media, Inc.; Shutterstock
Interior Photographs: Alamy, AP Images, iStockphoto, Shutterstock

Publisher's Cataloging-in-Publication Data

Names: Polinsky, Paige V., author.
Title: Tunnels / by Paige V. Polinsky.
Description: Minneapolis, MN : Abdo Publishing, 2018. | Series: Engineering super structures.
Identifiers: LCCN 2016962868 | ISBN 9781532111068 (lib. bdg.) | ISBN 9781680788914 (ebook)
Subjects: LCSH: Tunnels--Juvenile literature. | Tunnels--Design and construction--Juvenile literature. | Civil engineering--Juvenile literature.
Classification: DDC 624--dc23
LC record available at http://lccn.loc.gov/2016962868

SandCastle™ Level: Fluent

SandCastle™ books are created by a team of professional educators, reading specialists, and content developers around five essential components—phonemic awareness, phonics, vocabulary, text comprehension, and fluency—to assist young readers as they develop reading skills and strategies and increase their general knowledge. All books are written, reviewed, and leveled for guided reading, early reading intervention, and Accelerated Reader™ programs for use in shared, guided, and independent reading and writing activities to support a balanced approach to literacy instruction. The SandCastle™ series has four levels that correspond to early literacy development. The levels are provided to help teachers and parents select appropriate books for young readers.

EMERGING • BEGINNING • TRANSITIONAL • FLUENT

CONTENTS

About Tunnels

Tunnels are **passageways**.
They run through earth or rock.

Some run **underground**. Others
pass through mountains.

Some tunnels are very old. One is in Iraq. It runs under the Euphrates River.

It is 4,000
years old!

Ancient tunnels were
used in many ways.

Some carried water to crops or cities. Others were walking paths.

Many tunnels carry water today.
Others are used for **mining**.
Miners dig deep tunnels.

Miners gather metals and **minerals** from these tunnels.

Today's tunnels are used for travel too. Trains and cars pass through mountain tunnels.

Subway trains travel in **underground** tunnels. People travel across busy cities in the trains.

The Channel Tunnel runs under
the sea. It connects England
and France.

This tunnel is
often called
the Chunnel.

15

Engineers plan tunnels carefully.
They study the area's soil and rocks.

They build tunnels with strong
materials. Most tunnels are made
of **concrete** and **steel**.

Workers dig tunnels using many
tools. Tunnel boring machines dig
through soft rock.

Explosives break up harder rock.

Workers wash tunnel walls.
They also check the tunnel's
air flow.

This keeps tunnels safe and clean.

Think About It

Many tunnels are used for travel.
How else do people use tunnels?

GLOSSARY

concrete – a mixture of sand, gravel, cement, and water that becomes hard when it dries.

engineer – someone who is trained to design and build structures such as machines, cars, or roads.

explosive – a substance used to blow up something.

material – the substance something is made of, such as metal, fabric, or plastic.

mineral – a natural substance found in the earth that does not come from an animal or plant.

mining – digging up materials from underground.

passageway – a long narrow space that allows you to pass from one place to another.

steel – a strong, hard metal made from iron.

underground – below the surface of the earth.